Mike Riddell was a prolific writer of fiction, nonfiction, poetry, screenplays and plays. Born and bred in New Zealand, he was, in addition to his work as a writer, a lecturer in theology at New Zealand's southernmost university, a regular columnist for *Third Way* magazine, a filmmaker, an environmentalist, and a mentor to others in many ways.

For all the blokes brave enough to go to the doctor.

Mike Riddell

WONKY PONK DOWN UNDER

One Man's Journey Through
Prostate Cancer

AUSTIN MACAULEY PUBLISHERS®

LONDON * CAMBRIDGE * NEW YORK * SHARJAH

A CIP catalogue record for this title is available from the British Library.

ISBN 9781035890781 (Paperback)
ISBN 9781035890798 (ePub e-book)

www.austinmacauley.com

First Published 2025
Austin Macauley Publishers Ltd®
1 Canada Square
Canary Wharf
London
E14 5AA

Table of Contents

Chapter 1
Revelations

My GP is attractive and extremely vivacious. I've had dinner with her and her entrepreneurial husband. She's funny and compassionate. But right now, she's wriggling her rubber-gloved finger up my anus in a somewhat discomforting manner. I doubt she enjoys it any more than I do, or that we'll be having a return dinner engagement anytime soon.

I'm facing the wall, pretending that it's quite common for people to apply gel and explore my rectum. In truth, I'm struggling with the fact that the probing is producing a sensation similar to the prelude to defecation, an outcome that could prompt a messy ending to our friendship.

Finally, it's over, and I'm allowed to retrieve my clean underpants and my soiled dignity.

"Well," she tells me, "I can't feel anything out of the ordinary."

I'm not sure whether to feel relieved or insulted. I opt for taking a chair opposite her, thereby planting my nether regions safely out of danger of further violation.

I remind myself that most women of my age will have had any number of medical men inserting fingers and cold steel implements in their vaginas without charges being laid.

"Just the same, we'll need to get the urinary problems sorted," my doctor says.

I nod, but not too vigorously, for fear that mention of urine combined with movement rippling through my bladder might provoke a sudden leakage. It's my old man's problem with peeing that has me making this rare visit to the lovely physician.

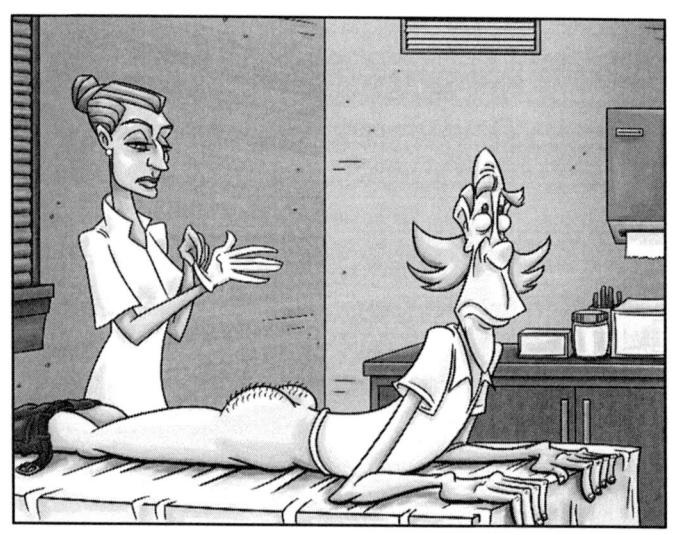

My PSA score has been creeping up. A few months ago, it was 8; now it's 9.4. I've always been of the opinion that a higher score is better than a lower one in any human endeavour, so I've been relatively chuffed at the trend. Apparently, I'm out of step with medical opinion on this.

"I imagine it's BPH," I opine, demonstrating my knowledge of the acronym for benign prostate hyperplasia and simultaneously my dexterity in using Google for self-diagnosis.

She gives me her practised frown for bush doctors, one eyebrow slightly arched.

"I've done a referral for the urology department at the hospital," she says. "With a bit of luck, they might give you a rebore."

She laughingly explains that rebore is a specialised medical term for what we laypeople might call a transurethral resection of the prostate, or TURP. I nod wisely. My brother had a rebore done on his 1952 twin-spinner Chevvy after it did a piston ring. So I'm not completely ignorant of such matters. In fact, a piston and a piss tin are not completely dissimilar.

It looks like I'm destined for further investigation at the hands of our public health system.

Chapter 2
Into the Breach

The appointment comes two months later. A letter instructs me to proceed to our local hospital's urology department.

Somewhat appropriately, the service is located deep in the bowels of the hospital. On this day, ironically, it is temporarily closed because of sewerage problems. I'm redirected.

I've been instructed to drink copious amounts of water in the hours leading up to my appointment—a dangerous experiment for someone with a bladder like mine. But it's needed because I'm about to have a flow test.

The process involves peeing into a toilet bowl with some sort of measuring device attached that records both the quantity and velocity of my urine stream. As I'm dribbling into the electronic latrine, a printer beside it chatters out the results in real time. I give it my best, which I fear is less than adequate.

I return to an adjacent room, where a nurse rubs my lower abdomen with gel and performs an ultrasound. What is it with gel in medical practice? Medicos must be the best consumers of KY around. Apparently, the point of the procedure is to examine my bladder and see what's left in there.

I'm shunted back to the waiting room and eventually called for a session with a man in a white coat. He's an enthusiastic Chinese man who reveals his status as a registrar. We end up in a small consulting room, where he admits he's not done much of this sort of medicine before.

He has a form with numerous questions on it, and we work our way through it. I do my best to be candid about my abysmal performance in the toilet arena. He shuffles through the paperwork and eventually finds the results of the recent flow test.

He looks at me with due scepticism and suggests I try to do better next time. I feel a little chastised, despite my secret knowledge there's no better available.

We then arrive at that time we both know is inevitable. He instructs me to lie down on the bed, lower my pants and turn to face the wall. I do so and listen to the sound of rubber gloves snapping. At this point, the registrar realises he can't find any gel and goes looking for some. The room I'm in must be the only one in the entire hospital without it. I'm left for five minutes with my rear end facing the door, hoping no one calls in to say hello.

My man returns with gel and proceeds to join the throng who've already found interest in probing my rectum. After several minutes of investigation, he mutters to himself and turns back to his computer, having mercifully removed the gloves.

Mumbling to himself and his screen, he consults it for wisdom. I eventually roll over onto my back, feeling a little neglected, and observe him researching prostate on Doctor Google. I recognise some of the pages I looked up in the week preceding the appointment. His online scrutiny does not fill me with confidence.

After some time with the oracle and a few questions about my symptoms, he turns to face me. He agrees that the prostate is a problem. There are two possible ways forward, he suggests. One would be an MRI to clarify what's going on; the other would be the rebore I was hoping to get. He seems uncertain, and I get the feeling he'd flip a coin if I weren't present.

After a considerable amount of umming and aahing, he disappears down the corridor to speak with his supervising consultant, again leaving me stranded still with my pants down. A nurse calls in at one stage, realises she's in the wrong room, and hurriedly departs.

I hang on in there with my sail in the wind until the plucky registrar finally returns with a decision. A biopsy will be performed with the intention of seeing if a TURP is the best treatment.

He gets me to sign a consent form, even though my nether regions continue to remain exposed. The medical team needs to be certain that I'm not harbouring a certain antibiotic-resistant infection. He'll need to take a swab, he informs.

I nod and open my mouth. But it seems the swab is destined for an orifice further south.

Finally, I'm allowed to reclothe myself and gather my dignity, or what's left of it. The registrar gives me a cheery smile and wishes me on my way.

Chapter 3
Just a Little Prick

A couple of weeks on, I find my way to Waikato Hospital urology department for another appointment. The receptionist tells me the urologist I'm to see is still caught up with an urgent operation and there will be a delay. Given my urinary performance, I'm used to delays.

The urologist eventually turns up, panting from his brisk walk from the operating theatre. He disappears into his office, while I'm admitted to the inner chambers. There, a nurse confirms my details and gets me to lower my trousers for the inevitable.

Once I'm suitably disrobed, the urologist enters. It's a strange introduction, with me facing the wall and him stretching his rubber gloves. He describes what's about to happen and then introduces an anaesthetic-bearing needle that I mercifully can't see.

He inserts it somewhere in my anus, with the vaguely disconcerting words, "Just a little prick."

The needle is soon replaced with what I can only assume is some sort of ultrasound, intended to measure my offending prostate. He informs the nurse that the prostate's volume is 68.3 cubic centimetres. Something in his voice suggests to me that this size might be above average. I experience a brief flush of pride. He continues to probe around in there with his finger, following the road most travelled.

But things are about to get worse. The next piece of equipment to be introduced is the biopsy needle itself. I can't see it, of course, but for all the world it sounds like someone has shoved a stapler up my arse and is enjoying operating it.

While all this is taking place, the urologist chats away to me about the film script I'm writing. It's about a New Zealand plastic surgeon by the name of Sir Archibald (Archie) McIndoe. The urologist takes a keen interest in all this and tells me he still uses surgical instruments that McIndoe invented. Not the same ones, I trust, given McIndoe invented them decades earlier.

Finally, it's over. I'm allowed to pull up my pants and to see the consultant face to face. He tells me I'll get the results in a couple of weeks or so.

I drive home, and as the anaesthetic wears off, I find my bottom end a tad painful. It's not helped by the fact that for the next week or so I'll find myself pissing blood—an effect I have admittedly been warned about in advance.

I'm feeling a little impatient for the hospital to confirm the fact that my prostate is bloated but non-malignant so they can get on with scheduling a rebore and provide me with some relief.

But nothing in the world of public health moves fast, other than the turnover of patients.

Chapter 4
Pizzle-Rot

Three weeks pass before I return to the labyrinthine corridors of the hospital to get my results. I'm very relaxed about it all. This time the urology department is open for business and the urologist is apparently onsite.

I'm therefore a tad bemused to find both the waiting room and the nearby corridor packed with customers. It seems we've all been summoned at the same time. The only solution is to hurry up and wait. I manage to find a chair and settle in with my Kindle that I've had the foresight to bring along.

An hour and a half later than my allotted appointment time, I'm summoned by name. I enter another cubicle, currently occupied by a youthful-looking urologist and a student in the last year of her medical training. I unintentionally check my trouser belt to see if it's fastened.

The urologist greets me breezily, and I sit and prepare myself for what I already know—I have an enlarged prostate and will need the aforementioned rebore.

The specialist rather wrong-foots me with the encouraging news that he doesn't think my cancer has spread too far. It occurs to me that he's possibly mixed up my results with someone else's.

I must have looked just a little startled because he soothes me with the statistic that 30 percent of men my age have some level of prostate cancer.

Nevertheless, he wants to get an MRI and a bone scan done to check that the cancer hasn't spread to other parts of my body.

"Ah yes," I say learnedly, keen to demonstrate my thorough research into this form of cancer. "I understand that most men die *with* prostate cancer rather than *of* it."

The urologist looks at me as if I'm a testicle short of a full package and throws in a censorious frown.

"That's not the case with you," he rules. "This is an aggressive and fast-moving form of cancer. You'll die from it if it's not treated."

He tells me I have two options. One is a radical prostatectomy, which involves surgically removing the offending organ. This approach would have the added advantage of curing my urinary reticence.

The other is radiation treatment, which is less invasive but has the side effect of actually slowing up my ability to piss. Any further delay would force me to use my penis as a drinking straw, which is not something I find appealing.

The doctor hands me a booklet about prostate cancer and tells me I'll receive a letter about my next appointment. With that, I'm dismissed. Ten minutes ago, I needed a minor medical procedure. Now, it seems, I'm a cancer patient.

I know I'll need some time to grasp the concept.

On the trudge back down the endless hallway, I consider whether I should tell my wife or not. To do so would only make her worry. But then I figure she'll guess something is up anyway, just by looking at my face. She won't need a finger up my bum to realise what's troubling me.

So I sit in my car and text her.

Not such a good result, I tell her. *There's a bit of cancer in the prostate.*

I'm trying to break it gently, not quite believing the news myself.

When she gets home from work, we hug for a few minutes. Forty-three years of marriage ensures we don't always need to use words to convey our feelings.

Momentarily, the future looks bleak. Then I tell her that I've decided to name my affliction pizzle-rot—a condition that affects the ability of male sheep to gain an erection. We laugh in the face of death. I'm buggered if I'm going to get all maudlin about it.

After a lot of talking and a quick dinner, we head over to the house of some good friends. They have another couple, who are also dear friends of ours, staying with them for the night.

Unbowed, I tell them of my pizzle-rot, and we drink a celebratory glass of champagne in honour of life. The male half of our host couple has survived ten years since he was treated for prostate cancer. This reminder is very encouraging.

But the other couple are on their way down-country for a close relative's funeral. He'd died a couple of days ago from, you guessed it, prostate cancer.

Caught between these two possible outcomes, we nonetheless have a wonderful night of laughing and recounting stories. If you're going to have cancer, you might as well celebrate your life and humanity in the presence of people who love you.

Then, at 3 a.m., I find myself awake contemplating the prospect that I might die. The shadow of death doesn't frighten me, but I know my wife will be mightily pissed off at me if I do shuffle off. And she's a force to be reckoned with.

This will be the first of many nights when the dark hours bring doubts and anxieties, probing my cavalier defences. It's like the cancer itself—seeking out vulnerabilities to exploit.

I meditate on my father, a survivor of jaw cancer, several major strokes, his own prostate surgery, a ruptured spleen, and a severed optical nerve. He's 92 years old, still smoking, as he has done all his life, and living alone in his own house. The personification of stubbornness, my dad teaches me the value of it.

If he can do it, so can I.

Chapter 5
Ironman

I'm scheduled for an MRI. The radiology department is a bit overloaded with clients, but they decide to run an evening clinic to fit us all in. There's that nagging anxiety of the ticking clock, so I'm well-pleased to get an appointment.

I follow the instructions to get to the right place, and with my daughter's assistance (my wife is away in Wellington), I trek along the silent corridors. There's a minor hiccup when we find our way barred by a locked door but we soon manage our way around it to our destination.

Over the entrance, there's a large sign announcing Regional Cancer Centre. For the first time, it sinks in that I really am a cancer patient. In my younger days, I always wondered what I'd be when I grew up, and now I know. It's nothing I ever anticipated. My high school career adviser didn't raise cancer patient as a potential avenue of advancement.

I settle into my new vocation of waiting and eventually am summoned to the chambers of the MRI lab. I'm instructed to strip off, don a loose-fitting robe, and make sure I have nothing metal about my person. It's times like this that you're grateful you're not Ironman.

Following the guidance of the technician, I climb up onto a fairly comfortable white bed so that I'm facing the entrance of what looks like the gateway to the Large Hadron Collider.

My man in the white coat covers me with what appears to be a metal door, but he describes it as an antenna. It weighs heavily on me, and I suspect its main purpose is to keep me still. There's an intercom in the machine. He asks me what radio station I'd like to listen to.

"Something relaxing," I say.

And with that, we're off, sliding gently into the mouth of the magnetic beast like a sacrificial virgin. Well, not so much of the virgin, really.

Unfortunately, the easy listening radio network is heading toward the end of the hour, so all I can hear are loud, jangling commercials. The technician asks me how I'm feeling as the claustrophobic lips swallow my head.

"All they're playing is ads," I complain.

"Can't do much about that," he replies.

I guess there's an inch between the end of my nose and the roof of the tunnel. I close my eyes and think of England. Super conscious not to spoil the whole thing by moving, I unsuccessfully try to stop my diaphragm from doing its breathing thing.

A series of beeps, clicks, and whirs occurs throughout the procedure, as if R2D2 has somehow made it onto set. Every now and again, the bed moves me along the gullet of the machine.

Toward the end of the process, a vigorous shaking and banging starts up. I try not to imagine that the whole giant apparatus is about to self-destruct, but apparently it's perfectly normal. I'm gently expelled from my host's throat and told I can dismount.

"Wow," I say to the radiologist. "That's some crazy carnival ride you've got going there."

He blinks at me.

"Never heard it called that before," he says.

Well, I've never ridden one like that before.

The medical community now knows more about my body than I do. I wish I could have a copy of the scan to use for my profile picture.

Freshly dressed and keen to get out of the place, I collect my daughter from the waiting room and we repair to a burger joint in order to decontaminate ourselves. There we eat and laugh and luxuriate in the close family bond that binds us.

As we drive home afterwards, rain sets in. For some reason, I'm distracted and fail to give way on a roundabout. I slam on the brakes and come within inches of a major collision. It would be ironic to die on the way home from cancer treatment. I really must pay attention.

Chapter 6
Dem Bones, Dem Bones,
Dem Dry Bones

Next up, bone scan—to make sure the cancer hasn't snuck its way into the marrow of my skeleton while I wasn't watching. My lovely wife gets time off work to accompany me.

The process is a two-stage one. First up is an injection of some sort of radioactive material, which apparently finds its way into my bones. You might be forgiven for feeling a bit dubious when someone offers not only to expose you to radiation but also to inject it into your veins. And here's me thinking New Zealand is a nuclear-free zone.

I joke that the radiologists won't need any sort of machine for this one. No doubt my bones will light up like a Christmas tree and set off any Geiger counters in the immediate vicinity.

Anyway, it seems this is not an accurate understanding of the procedure involved. I'm told to go away for three hours, during which time I'm free to eat and drink and then return for the next stage of the examination. The prisoner's last meal, perhaps. My wife, never one to miss an opportunity, suggests we go shopping.

On returning to the scene of the crime at the appointed hour, I'm summoned into a room that is helpfully adorned with radiation warning symbols. I get to strip off and wear one of the powder-blue hospital robes that has seen good service.

I'm asked to climb onto another bed at the jaws of another machine. I'm not quite tied to it, but straps are affixed to my elbows and ankles to prevent unauthorised movements. These procedures must be very attractive to fetishists.

The radiologist warns me that the proactive part of the apparatus will get very close to my face when the team begins scanning my skull. No doubt they're checking to see if it's hollow or not.

I try not to panic as something resembling a laundry press descends from above, grinding with robotic intent. It stops barely an inch from my nose and hovers menacingly. I close my eyes and imagine I'm not being irradiated.

The bed slides its way through the tunnel in programmed tranches, and I'm processed like so much salami. I pretend to myself that the bed's a sunbed, and that the warmth I'm feeling probably isn't nuclear fission in my bone marrow.

Just when I think the process has almost ended, the radiologist approaches with a concerned frown. She asks if I'd mind lowering my underwear, which I've thus far been allowed to keep on as a token of modesty.

I tell her I'm a married man, but she insists. Her explanation that there's something she can't quite see does little for my masculine pride. I feel like informing her that the part in question is boneless. But being a compliant soul, I lower my boxers and submit.

Another five minutes, and it's all over. I collect my clothes and dignity and rejoin my wife. Someone should implement a loyalty card scheme for hospital procedures—10 stamps on a card and—bingo—a free colonoscopy.

Chapter 7
Tiffany

If I were in the United States, it would be my wallet rather than my skeleton that was being scanned. I'd be battling insurance companies who would argue that they have no liability because of my prostate's pre-existing condition and its probable damage from over-exuberant sexual activity.

I give thanks that I live in a country with a functioning public health system, staffed by professionals.

One of them is Tiffany, who has the title of urogenital cancer nurse. I assume she doesn't introduce herself that way at parties. But she becomes my inside man, so to speak.

Tiffany is the one who has pushed to get my scans done before my wife and I embark on a long-planned trip to Panama. She doorsteps the doctors and passes on information through a clandestine dead drop subterfuge. Actually, she just emails it, but I'm grateful anyway.

Against the odds, she has arranged for my file to appear before the weekly gathering of wise heads at their review meeting—a mere day after my bone scan! Here the genital giants ponder how to proceed with cases such as mine.

Knowing we're about to fly out a few days after the meeting, Tiffany chalks the side of a newspaper stand, and I pick up the results of my tests. They turn out to be something of a curate's egg—coincidentally about the same size and shape as my prostate.

There's no cancer in my bones, which I imagine is better than the alternative. And that which is brewing in my nether regions is reasonably localised, though it may have seeped into my seminal vessels. I imagine these are the aircraft carriers of sperm jets, but I could be wrong.

One disconcerting aspect is that my Gleason score (named after Donald, whose father ran a hardware store) is 5+5=10. Given that 10 is the highest possible score, I congratulate myself on getting full marks. But I soon realise I've indulged in another misguided celebration.

My pizzle-rot is aggressive. Well, I can be aggressive when I want to. You should see my version of "Who're you looking at, punk?" It strikes fear into blind chihuahuas.

What my score actually means is…who knows? The feeling of the review committee is that there are several options. Like dying or not dying. Of the two, I'm leaning toward the latter.

A meeting with the specialist is scheduled for when we return from Panama. In the meantime, Tiffany advises me to have a good holiday, enjoy being with family, and not to worry about anything.

That's a prescription I can live with. Do I have to declare on my immigration form to the US that I'm carrying cancer, or is it just Korans they're worried about?

For 11 days, I'm able to keep my thoughts above my belt. My wife and I jet off to Panama for our son's wedding, which happily coincides with his 40th birthday. It's a time of joy and celebration, and my prostate is happy to relax for a moment.

The combination of eating, drinking, laughing, and being together is just the tonic I need. I like to think the cancer cells are taking a break and sipping sangria.

The word 'cancer' is the equivalent of pissing in a baptismal font. It comes with more freight than a long-haul locomotive. We're all scared of it, like the monster that lives under the bed. Okay, that's enough mixed metaphors for now.

My mother, whose parents both died from 'the big C', always wanted me to find a cure for cancer when I grew up. Bugger. I knew there was something I forgot to do. Might have been handy about now. Instead, I frittered my time away, learning how to love life. Stupid, I know. But here in the soft warmth of Panama City, drinking Laphroaig with my son and his new wife, I feel I could have done worse things with my time.

Chapter 8
ED

Nothing quite like the trek down the convoluted corridors of the urology department dungeon to bring one back to earth.

I feel like a reluctant Labrador dragged into the vet's rooms, skidding across the vinyl floor with the smell of raw animal fear proving less than inviting. My wife and I take our vinyl-covered chairs alongside all the others waiting for Godot-knows-what.

I have my trusty Kindle but find myself reading the same paragraph over and over again. I guess it's one way of making the book seem longer.

Finally, a nurse calls my name. She regrets informing me that the doctor requires a flow test before he can see me. I point out to her that it might have been helpful if I'd known this a little earlier, given that one of the requirements for a flow test is to consume a litre of water three hours beforehand.

She's sympathetic but insistent. I quickly down two glasses of water, summon my resolve, and head to the cyber pisspot. There I labour away for some time before the sensor even cares enough to begin chattering. I fear this pathetic dribble will not impress anyone.

Finally, my wife and I are admitted to the Holy of Holies, the consulting room. Except that it has the aura of a hall closet that has been renovated to make a well-used smokers' area.

We're here, so we've been told, to learn of my recommended treatment plan. By way of preparation, we've been reading everything we can get our hands on concerning possible plans of attack, together with potential side-effects. All of them include erectile dysfunction (ED). If you factor in death, the outcome remains the same, unless you have faith in the resurrection.

I may have many deficiencies, some more obvious than others. But standing to attention when the occasion demands has never been one of them. There have been no misfires with my erectile projectile. I can launch at the drop of a hat or, more accurately, the drop of a pair of knickers.

It seems I have the choice between becoming a literal or chemical member of the castrati. This is not a winning inducement in the promotional stakes for curing pizzle-rot.

Did I mention that my wife is a judge? Having spent some time scribbling on her legal pad, she has developed a line of cross-examination that entails 23 questions for the unsuspecting consultant. I'm surprised she hasn't asked for a verified copy of his credentials.

The doctor at hand is a pleasant chap. He dismisses my flow test as well below the failure grade. I'm reminded of a joke about an Irishman who asks his physician what a specimen is. When the medical man replies, "Piss in a cup," the patient retorts, "Shit in a hat," and the fight's on.

Then there's another one about a Kiwi in London who's on his way to watch the All Blacks play at Twickenham. He gets run down by a car. When he wakes up in hospital, he's told the surgeons will have to remove his testicles. Greatly concerned about this bleak prospect, he asks for a second opinion.

Another physician is wheeled in, but after a thorough examination agrees with the initial assessment. Even more deeply concerned, the man asks if there's a Kiwi doctor available to take a look.

They manage to find one. The doctor consults the notes and has a look at the affected area.

"Sorry, mate, we're going to have to whip your balls out."

Unexpectedly, the injured man grins.

"Thank Christ for that!" he exclaims. "I thought those Pommy bastards said they were gonna take me test tickets."

Meanwhile, our consultant is calling up the results of my MRI on his computer screen. He points out the malignant areas of my prostate with enthusiasm. We stare blankly at an image that looks like a cross between a Rorschach ink blot and a paisley tie. I feel like asking if he can tell the gender.

Under a persistent line of questioning from my judicial spouse, he cracks and admits he's not yet sure if the cancer has spread into the lymph nodes. All he can testify to is that the situation is 'suspicious'—a claim my wife dismisses as hearsay.

The crucial relevance of this point goes to whether my prostate can be surgically extracted, thus bringing to a sad demise the rude cancer cells, or whether it is too late for that, and some other method of attack is indicated.

At this point, the recalcitrant specialist offers a fresh possibility. There is a bright, shiny new scan available, known as a PSMA PET-CT scan. I'm momentarily offended that he's suggesting a canine clinic. But he explains this procedure will identify every last molecular particle of prostate cancer in my body and where it's hiding. Sort of like US surveillance satellites.

There are two drawbacks. The procedure is only available in Auckland, and it costs $3000. A quick glance between my wife and I confirms that we'd rather have our wallet lightened than my pelvis, should we encounter such a choice. Knowledge is power when it comes to health.

Having acknowledged this point, the irrepressible judge continues to probe for any imprecise language in the physician's testimony, but eventually allows him to stand down.

We leave none the wiser as to what I might be facing but cheered by the prospect of more accurate information. Within the hour, there's a phone call to confirm my appointment for the doggy scan at the suitably named Mercy Hospital, just a few days hence. I'm up for all the mercy I can get.

During the drive home, we ring my wife's mother, an 88-year-old widow. She's full of support, but near the end of the conversation she has just one question. Will treatment affect our sex life? On learning that sadly the answer is yes, she gives us some sage advice. Count the days you have left to indulge, and have at it, she counsels. I always did respect my elders.

Chapter 9
Scanned or Scammed?

The chances of surviving prostate cancer are roughly equivalent to those of surviving Auckland traffic. We drive up to the city from Hamilton the night before the scan and stay in a cheap motel near the hospital in the interests of making the 8 a.m. appointment. By the time we arrive in Auckland, we're ready for dinner.

The motel promises a restaurant, but it turns out to be a shallow boast. We enter the tawdry establishment, which seems as empty as a Galilean tomb. A sullen man with a grubby apron emerges from the kitchen to tell us he's busy because he has an order.

He waves us toward our choice of any table we like, given there are no other patrons. We sit at what appears to be the sort of table previously found in orphanages or homes for unmarried mothers. My wife and I peruse the meagre menu and look at each other bravely. Perhaps hardship is to be our lot from hereon.

But I look around, raise my eyebrows, and stand. Like naughty schoolchildren, we sneak out of the chop shop, not wishing to raise the ire of the cook, who no doubt has a range of knives handy.

Down the road we wander and light upon a very acceptable Indian restaurant, which is actually worthy of the description. It sets me up nicely for the next morning, which involves water-only fasting.

Having survived the night, we allow ourselves 30 minutes to drive to the nearby hospital. The journey takes five minutes. As a result, the designated reception area we usher ourselves into is otherwise empty. A radio is playing some inane chatter. We take our seats and thumb through magazines, wondering if there has been a radiation leak.

After some time, a technician emerges from a door and looks nonplussed to find customers. She explains that the receptionist must be sick. Would we mind paying for the procedure after instead of before my scan? I reckon I can live with that, so long as I live through it.

When the technician finishes arranging her lunch in the fridge, she leads me to a small room containing a large armchair and a television. She runs through the coming procedure with me. After I've changed into a hospital gown, which I soon discover is rather more stylish than public hospital ones, I'll be injected, via a shunt in my arm, with gallium—apparently not French courage but a radioactive substance.

I'll then need to wait an hour. I calculate 60 minutes of waiting works out financially as $25 per minute—not that I'm counting—during which time I'll be given a bottle of water to drink and endeavour to empty my bladder as much as possible. (Contradictory advice, in my opinion.) I'll also be given a newspaper to read, which I anticipate doing in a leisurely fashion.

Once the hour is up, two large syringes full of chlorine will be whacked up my veins—presumably to enhance my white honky status.

I duly allow these phases of the procedure to play out, until finally I'm ushered into another room, where another white doughnut machine awaits, along with another injection.

I'm a little disconcerted, however, that the technician administering it does so from behind a lead shield.

Another technician asks me to lie on the bed. I comply, aiming my head for the pillows, only to be informed I'm upside down. If your feet smell and your nose runs, you're built upside down. Once that little problem is sorted, the technician covers me with a blanket. Very thoughtful. Then he sellotapes my head to the bed. Not so thoughtful.

The next instruction sent my way requires me to stretch my arms over my head, at which point my friendly technician leans in and secures both of my arms with a belt around the elbows. The binding is necessary, he says, to keep my arms from touching the sides of the machine. Not that they really care about my elbows, he explains; they just don't want me damaging the equipment.

From here on in, everyone vacates the room in a vaguely disturbing hurry, and my bed moves into the giant white vagina. It spins and hums to itself in self-indulgent pleasure. I close my eyes and subject myself to the will of the robotic mind.

Thirty minutes later, it's all over, and I'm expelled like a spent piece of gum. My shunt is removed from behind the lead barrier. I'm instructed not to have contact with pregnant women or children for a few hours. Then I'm allowed to get dressed again and rejoin my wife.

The final treatment involves a delicate medical procedure known as draining my credit card. This is the only painful part of the appointment, but I put on a brave face.

Chapter 10
Hot Spots

Before leaving the hospital, I engage in some discussion with the authorities about getting the results of this latest test. It seems to me that (a) it's my body they've been scanning, and (b) I'm paying for the procedure. To my mind, it follows (c) that I should get the results delivered to me. But this logical sequence is not the way they see things.

There is a PROTOCOL (not to be confused with a procto-tool) that dictates a patient should only receive their results in the presence of a medical professional. I suppose I could play my doctor card, but a PhD in religious studies probably won't fool them for long. They tell me to talk to my GP, who should receive the report sometime in the following week.

Not being someone who welcomes subservience, I instead email my girl Tiffany, explaining that it would be helpful to me to know how deeply the rot has corroded my pizzle.

Once again, by the end of the next day, she comes through for me—*with the information*, for those of you with grubby minds.

She rings to tell me that the suspicion surrounding my lymph nodes is unfounded. There are no "hot" spots apart from the prostate and seminal vesicles. I'm lymph with relief.

The results have been examined by two radiologists, and they've both given me the all-clear for that particular part of my anatomy.

There are two reasons for celebration. One is that the cancer has not yet spread much of anywhere else. The second is that what is there could potentially be dealt with by a relatively straightforward prostatectomy rather than radiation. I'm feeling like my rad level is pretty much elevated already, and I don't mean this in a cool way.

Which way will my pizzle swing? Unfortunately, it will be another 11 days before my next appointment and I can find out. I trust that in the meantime my prostate will behave itself and restrain any ambitions to annex other territories.

In the interim, I compose a two-page essay to the medical powers that be, outlining my opinions in terms of a preferred avenue of treatment. I'm sure they're dazzled by my newfound status as an oncologist and are ready to defer their years of training to my dexterity with Google. Later, the more rational side of my brain recognises that they've probably filed my words in a round container under a desk.

And so it is that my wife and I find ourselves seated once again in the long corridor leading to the gates of Hades. The linoleum hall is packed with sad old bastards like me, swapping war stories of their urinary engagements. The wait this time is only 100 minutes, which in the scheme of things is the blink of an eye.

Finally, my name is called, and we're ushered beyond the veil to the tawdry rooms that pass for the inner sanctum. My face lights up somewhat when I see that my consultant this time is the same chap who had the stapler up my arse during what passed for a biopsy.

And to our mutual delight, the lovely Tiffany has arranged to be present. She is the fount of all knowledge, and it's very reassuring to have her there.

Chapter 11
Eternal Flaccidity

The medical consultation begins with a return to discussing my film project about Archie McIndoe, the script of which has recently been greenlit and is currently being sold in Cannes. My man with the stapler, Glen, is a real enthusiast. He tells me that just a few weeks ago he was driving along listening to a podcast about McIndoe.

An unfortunate pause in our cinematic zeal allows the conversation to sink below the belt. With gregarious passion, Glen congratulates me on the fact that the PET scan has found no evidence of distemper. Similarly, he informs me that there is no indication of prostate cancer outside the general capsule. This, he assures me, is very good news. It means they can get on with surgery, which has been the outcome I hoped for. Get rid of the bloody thing and the cancer with it! Excellent. I'm a happy chappie.

In the very next breath, he tells me I'll be permanently impotent. We need to go wide, he explains, with all the fervour of a half-back eyeing his wing from the base of the scrum. He demonstrates with his hands, indicating a breadth that would clean out my hipbones as well. I think he might be engaging in hyperbole.

I'd been expecting erectile dysfunction, as per the textbooks—but temporary, not enduring. Glen is unflinching in his honesty. He can guarantee that the only thing that will be rising following the surgery is my age.

The good judge is sideswiped by this news. I see that faint tremor that suggests tears might be near the surface. I'm not exactly overjoyed by the prospects of eternal flaccidity myself. I droop in anticipation.

There are possibilities, assures my wingman. Such as an injection that can be applied to the base of the penis to achieve an erection. But stabbing myself with a sterilised needle in an organ packed with pain receptors doesn't really appeal to me as foreplay.

It seems that the choice is between living with drastic side-effects or dying without them. The dilemma gives me pause for at least five seconds.

Glen goes on to outline other consequences of the prostatectomy, such as incontinence. Happily, however, these should be temporary. And they seem almost insignificant compared to my looming incapacity to rise to expectations.

I had been thinking of offering my doctor free tickets to the premiere of the film, provided I could achieve an erection before it happened. That would have required a nerve-sparing procedure. But now, it seems, the only things likely to be spared are wet dreams.

We book a date, my surgeon and me. Given the aggressive nature of my pizzle-rot (nah, *you,* fuck you!), I get the first available slot, some three weeks later. In public health terms, that's lightning quick. On the other hand, there are at least 21 days left for a ceremonial parade of my retiring member. I hear the faint strains of *The Last Post.*

The judge has recovered sufficiently to begin her cross-examination and proceeds with it. She asks whether perhaps the operation could be done under local rather than general anaesthesia. While I appreciate her probing acuity, the prospect of being awake through a four-hour operation while someone slices through various layers of my anatomy does little to excite me.

Eventually, the evidence-in-chief is finished, and I shake hands with my surgeon in the earnest hope that it won't be the last time. Tiffany collects the paperwork that needs completing. A few pages of questions to be answered and permissions to be given. The one about donating my soul to the devil gives me a slight pause, but needs must.

At least, I now have an appointment with destiny.

I recall the refrain from childhood games of hide and seek: "Coming, ready or not!"

Chapter 12
PSA

In the meantime, there's a meeting of the local prostate cancer support group. I'm not sure what to expect. Do we sit in a circle and confess? "My name's Mike, and I have pizzle-rot." Do we chant the prostate prayer? God grant me the tenacity to accept the cancer I didn't invite; courage to relinquish the virility I must; and wine to blur the consequences.

The gatherings happen only once every two months, so I take my chances and go. The meeting's being held in the privacy of an upstairs room of a local restaurant. There's no password needed, but nametags are provided. Inside, I discover a score of geriatric buggers like me, hovering around the bar to self-medicate.

The set-up looks like a jamboree for grumpy old men. Except they're more convivial than curmudgeonly, considering every last one of them is or has been struggling with cancer. I chat with a squat dairy farmer who advocates alternative therapy.

"I started with a PSA score of 1458," he tells me. "It was right through me, everywhere. After a few sessions with this guy, it came down to 900 odd," he enthuses.

And here was I thinking I'd topped the charts with 9.8. He's had his diagnosis for around three years, and to all appearances, he looks demonstrably alive. Something must be working for him.

We assemble around the table like a slightly expanded sitting of The Last Supper. The bloke who started the group with four members (now 30) just over a year ago summons us to order.

He begins reading the correspondence in the fashion of every business meeting I've ever attended—each item making my life seem longer than necessary. I find myself slipping into my default response of brain coma, counting the seconds by which my finite existence is slipping away.

Finally we get to the highlight of the evening—a proposed fundraising rugby match and auction for prostate cancer. Presumably, the goal is not to endorse prostate cancer as a desirable lifestyle option for affluent men but rather to provide funding for awareness campaigns and treatment.

A nuggetty chap who once played half-back takes over and spends the next half hour issuing guilt-inducing entreaties for volunteers to help organise the occasion. He'd make a good Catholic priest, and as a survivor of prostate surgery, he'd probably qualify as one.

I'm jolted back to consciousness by the invitation to new attendees to share a little of their story with the group. As much as anything to overcome the sensation that I have died quietly in the corner, I lead off and introduce myself.

"My name's Mike," I begin, before self-censoring.

I tell them how strange it is to become part of such a group, noting that I've never before been defined by an illness.

Several others follow, surprisingly eager to disclose the bare details of their encounter with an unwanted intruder. For the first time, it feels as if there's a degree of honesty and vulnerability in the room.

There's a guest speaker—a coach for high-performance athletes who's experienced six Olympic Games. He's younger than the rest of us, vibrant and interesting. He makes comparisons between the journey of an athlete and our own experience of dealing with cancer.

One of his insights is the need for a tight team (his term). He's not referring to the male package, or 'Little Richard and the twins', but to assembling a support group who will stay the distance. I guess endurance is a good quality both in the arena and the bedroom, even though our quest to breach the tape is sadly diminished.

The meals are served, and I chat to the guy next to me. He had a radical prostatectomy some four years back, but it didn't remove the cancer. The follow-up involved radiotherapy and hormone treatment. Now his PSA is back to near zero, and he's hopeful. I note that he swallows about 17 pills with his meal.

Am I looking into my future? Against the odds, I put my name down to volunteer for the fundraiser. It's for a good cause.

Chapter 13
Did You Hear the One About?

What is it about cancer that attracts alternative health nuts? No sooner do I announce my pizzle-rot than amateur physicians begin buzzing like flies around a steaming turd. On offer are diets, elixirs, therapies, and meditations, all accompanied by marvellous testimonies of guaranteed success.

They have a few things in common, these generous offers. All are suspicious of conventional medical science, imagining a giant conspiracy funded by Big Pharma. Growing up in New Zealand, I know a thing or two about big farmers and have found them remarkably uninterested in global domination and extremely well-educated on issues of pizzle-rot.

Also, very few of the apologists for a bright new disease-free future ask me for any details about my condition. All cancers are the same to them, and all can be attributed to unresolved psychic issues or contaminants in the food chain. They may be right, but at least my doctors offer me the respect of determining exactly what it is I'm suffering from.

I'm acutely aware of the mind–body continuum, in that my body doesn't seem to mind what I eat. But knowing I'm gestating a voracious cancer within persuades me toward trusting the verified understanding of medical staff who are no less humane or vested in healing than any enlightened sages who've just read a book I need to hear about. It's under the knife for me.

Chapter 14
Operation Knife

June 19 is a Monday. It's my appointment with fate. I'm to report to the hospital at 7 a.m., which means an early start to the day. The good judge drives me, and we pick up my daughter along the way. I know everything that is going to happen but have no idea what the experience will be like. I've never been fond of sharp instruments, and the thought of people rummaging around in my innards is unsettling.

The three of us find our way to the designated reception area, which resembles a crowded bus terminal. I thought I was special, but soon realise that I'm simply one of a throng assembled for surgery. Disconcertingly, the counter blinds are drawn down, even though we can all hear the staff chatting happily behind them.

We patients eye one another competitively, as if we're contestants in some sort of television show, anxious that others don't get special treatment. Eventually the blinds are retracted and a roll call ensues. After an anxious wait, my name is announced, and I'm allowed to join a queue to have my paperwork checked.

Yet another hospital gown is provided, together with a brown paper bag for all my worldly possessions. I have a choice between proceeding with treatment or sleeping rough. I'm invited to hop onto a bed so I can be wheeled through to the pre-op waiting room, where the former game show participants are lined up like planes on a runway. My wife and daughter are still with me. A nurse comes and sticks a shunt in my arm.

My surgeon turns up, bright and breezy. I ask him what sort of weekend he's had. I'm hoping he's not suffering from a throbbing hangover. He heads off to prep, and I remind him about my film that needs making and my desire to be around for it. Next up is a woman who is my anaesthetist. She's friendly and has impressive ink. She gives me a wee jab of something. Then a surgical registrar calls by to introduce himself, followed by a theatre nurse. So many attendants. It's like a living funeral.

The nurse spots the fact that I'm still wearing my Celtic cross around my neck and suggests I remove it. My daughter takes it from me and offers to wear it the entire time I'm in surgery and beyond. I'm touched by this act of love, while hoping she doesn't have ideas of preserving it from my impending cremation. We all say our goodbyes, and I'm wheeled into the operating theatre.

I note the bright lights and the buzz of activity. I'm feeling relaxed due to chemical assistance. There's another bed in the middle of the room, which I recognise as the operating table. I'm vaguely wondering how they're going to transfer me from one bed to the other and how many it will take to lift me.

I needn't have worried. The very next moment I'm waking up in the post-op recovery room. I glance across the room at a clock. It's 2.20 p.m. in the afternoon. I spend a few foggy moments trying to do the math in my head. The operation was supposed to be three hours or so. Have I been asleep since 11 a.m.? Did they actually do the op, or was I sent back for swearing at the staff in morphine-induced hallucinations? I am aware that I'm connected to a number of machines.

And then my surgeon is standing over me in godlike reassurance. It was a tough job, he says. The surgery took five and a half hours. The prostate was huge and growing around the bladder. He tells me that it was one of the most difficult dissections he's had to do in his entire career. I'm not sure whether to be proud or ashamed. Good to keep him on his toes, I guess, and it has to be a positive that I'm still here to get the report.

My wife and daughter are admitted, looking a tad anxious and wrung out. They'd waited a long time past the anticipated hour to get the surgeon's call. I suspect they're a bit miffed that I'm so chipper and positive, once again influenced by my chemical supplements. But all of us are delighted to be together on the other side of this ordeal—not that I have any memory of it whatsoever. With any luck, the cancer has been dealt to!

Chapter 15
Sliced and Diced

I am Mike's prostate. Nobody thinks about me in this story. Here I am just doing my thing, sprawling comfortably in the interior spaces without a care in the world. Then all of a sudden, I'm getting prodded, probed, stapled, and irradiated. Okay, so maybe I invaded a bit of space, but I go with the Israeli defence that there was no one living there anyway, so there was no harm. The stream that ran through my valley may have dried up a bit, but I hardly noticed.

Then, without warning, everyone goes nuclear on me. How come I'm the enemy? There may have been a few rogue elements living in the hills, but I'm hardly responsible for them. Why hold me guilty because they have plans for insurrection? I'm just enjoying my retirement, grateful that my services are not required as often as they were back in the day, sluicing seminal fluid like it was going out of fashion. If I take the odd day to smoke a cigarette on the veranda, what damage is done?

Without warning, I'm being cut into with sharp instruments. What can I do to fight back? I'm defenceless—the victim of an unprovoked attack. These invaders are heartless bastards. They're relentless, and they go for my near neighbours the seminal vesicles and lymph nodes as well. It's a scorched earth policy, turning our productive fields into barren waste. I'm sliced and diced and scraped out. What am I—chopped liver? Well yes, in fact I am. I was Mike's prostate, but that's all over now. So, it's over and out from me and back to Mike!

It's late afternoon before the hospital can summon an orderly from smoking out the back to wheel my bed up to the ward. I get a room next to the window, and if I squint really hard, I can see the lake! And there are only two beds in my suite, which initially sounds good.

I'm well and truly hooked up, in the medical sense of the term. There are tubes to siphon fluids into my body and other tubes to take fluids out. Best of all, there's a little button within reach, which turns out to be a pain pump. I'm hoping it's for the relief of pain rather than the stimulation of it.

I'm 'nil by mouth', an estimation shared by many of my critics over the years. I settle back into my bed, desiring only one thing—sleep.

Unfortunately, the man I'm sharing my room with, who is an anonymous voice behind a curtain, has other ideas. He's been in the hospital, nay, this very ward, several times before. He likes to think that the nurses remember him with fondness. They're too kind to disabuse him of this notion. The man has a daughter sitting with him who tactfully remains stoically silent.

There's no need for her to speak, because the man fills every acoustic space with words. He's the sort of person who has never had an unspoken thought in his life.

Every now and again he groans and exclaims, "Oh Jesus!" without any religious intent.

In between these regular punctuations, he papers the space with an inane monologue that invokes in me the sense of standing directly beneath a waterfall.

As darkness falls, he finally succumbs to sleep. The torrent of words is replaced with an apocalyptic snoring. My body eventually decides to switch off the acoustic assault from consciousness, and I plunge into sleep. Though not for long.

Chapter 16
Do Not Go Gentle into
That Good Night

Every hour through the night, nurses wake me to do their 'obs', as they call them. They empty my catheter bag and check my blood pressure. They ask me what my pain level is. My lovely room with a view turns out to be right next to the nurses' station. At some time during the night, I experience 'changeover'. One shift of nurses is finishing, and the other is starting. They overlap for what seems like an hour but may have been less.

The reason for this is to give them time to swap patient notes and developments. In reality, they use the time to talk about Facebook accounts, weekend parties, the weird quirks of doctors, holidays they've planned, and new clothes they've bought. I know this because they're all assembled outside the door of my room.

In time, I reach that stage of sleep deprivation when the CIA likes to do its best work. I don't know why they bother setting up rendition centres when there are hospitals in every major city.

My blood pressure is low. I know this because two Filipina nurses are very concerned about it, whispering to me in a spectral glow created by torchlight. They are a lovely pair, and I imagine they are sisters in the familial sense rather than the medical sense.

I promise to try to do better, without any idea how. The nurses increase the amount of fluid intake, consult the charts, and take my blood pressure on an hourly basis. I guess there's a basic scientific principle of 'fluid in, fluid out', as my catheter drain bag fills up alarmingly quickly. My two nocturnal angels are very attentive and caring. I sense their worry is a genuine one for my welfare. All I can think about is sleep in the absence of its presence.

Sometime just before dawn, my blood pressure begins to rise, which seems to be cause for celebration. It's probably going up because I'm contemplating how I might get out of bed to strangle my roommate.

The night passes like an endless trauma, and another shift changeover happens—marked by the equivalent of a hen's party outside my door. My patient-in-arms in the adjacent bed shifts from snoring to jabbering, a fair indication that he is awake.

They keep asking me what my pain level is on a scale of 10, and I routinely report that it's between 1 and 1.5. They look at me suspiciously, as if this is evidence of some sort of macho stoicism. But as far as I can estimate these things, it's the honest truth. Eventually, they remove the pain pump, which I've hardly used.

When breakfast arrives, I discover a new appreciation for my previous nil by mouth status. The only thing I'd been hanging out for is coffee. The coffee is instant, as I discover on my first taste. I choke on it and splutter so that it goes up my nose, no doubt helpfully scouring my nasal passage. Ah well, it provides a distraction from the incessant rabbiting that continues to fill the room.

Imagine if three talkback radio shows somehow end up broadcasting on one frequency, causing them to overlap unintelligibly. I don't need to imagine it. I'm there.

But what can I do about it? It's not like I can ring reception and complain about the guest who's making too much noise. I lie back and think of the Queen.

Chapter 17
Lemme Out of Here!

Earlier, the medical team promised me that if I behaved myself, I could get out on what will be the next day. No prisoner has ever felt more elated by the promise of release. It's consumed my every waking thought, and there are a lot of them. By now, pre-release day, I'm hallucinating with lines from Neil Young's song *After the Gold Rush* (1970) playing over and over in my head.

Well, I dreamed I saw the silver spaceships flying
In the yellow haze of the sun
There were children crying and colours flying
All around the chosen ones
All in a dream, all in a dream…

Meanwhile, I just keep swallowing the pills they give me without enquiring as to what they might be. I even attempt to consume some of the substance that passes for food, delivered with all the grace of a punch in the head. I'm determined to behave myself.

The judge comes in to sit with me, bringing her shining love that fills the room. And then, unexpectedly, Tiffany turns up, leaning against the wall with her laconic smile. She runs me through the mechanics of what has happened and what I can expect in the weeks to come.

The only bit I remember is that I'm not to attempt lifting anything that requires two arms for at least four weeks. She illustrates this warning with the story of a former patient who took this advice quite literally. Out of hospital for three weeks, he went pig hunting. Finding success, he sat looking at the porcine carcass, recalling the medical warning. With great Kiwi ingenuity, he devised a solution. He cut the beast into four pieces, which he proceeded to rope together. Then he placed the end of the rope over his shoulder and got on with the business of dragging the boar out of the bush. He wasn't lifting.

He ended up back in hospital, bewildered.

My final night on the ward is a comparative breeze. I achieve at least two hours' sleep.

After what is imaginatively described as breakfast has been cleared away, I hear a strange thunder. It sounds much like the annual migration of wildebeest. Finally, the herd bursts into my room, morphing into a chattering group of people in white coats. They arrange themselves around the end of my bed.

A consultant doctor takes my medical chart and hands it to a terror-stricken young woman. It's her responsibility to report my condition and progress to the rest of the team. She makes a fair job of it, even when some smart-arse guy who is a fellow registrar tries to throw her off course by challenging her summary.

The consultant asks some piercing questions about my blood pressure, and the eager beavers fight with one another to interject their theories. They look like blackbirds scrapping over a crust of bread. Eventually, of course, the guru consultant provides, with smug generosity, the enlightenment they've been striving toward.

And then, huffing like a street kid, my surgeon Glen arrives, apologising for his lateness. He brings a breeze of bonhomie, and we shake hands. It's strangely touching to be acknowledged as something other than a specimen.

He asks me about the buildup of gas in my bowel that he'd noted during surgery. I inform him that I've been farting like a draft horse, and he's enthusiastically pleased. The younger members of the posse look a tad discombobulated by this highly technical discussion.

Finally, the verdict is passed down to the accused. I am breathing and therefore a suitable candidate for discharge. Hallelujah!

The herd moves on to some other room, leaving the smiling figure of Tiffany, once again leaning against the wall. She gives me all the information I want, such as the exact time I can leave and what will happen once I'm home. A kind of streetwise Florence Nightingale, she is the bearer of the lamp.

Chapter 18
Extraction Team to the Rescue

I dress awkwardly, then text the good news of my impending release to the judge. She and my daughter and son-in-law turn up as part of the extraction team. We wait. And wait.

The problem, it seems, is my discharge papers. Or rather, the lack of them. A number of other patients are leaving the ward. Acknowledging that this has probably never before happened in the history of the hospital, I consider the unforeseen circumstance understandable.

But as I sit on and on in an uncomfortable chair, I become increasingly woozy and sore. My daughter, a social worker, goes over to the nurses' desk and leans on it, ready to practise her intimidation techniques gleaned from *The Sopranos.* The staff don't stand a chance.

They crack and agree that I can go and they'll post the papers should they ever reach a state of completion. Now free to leave, I find myself unable to. I need a wheelchair. And my son-in-law, who recently popped his Achilles tendon, also needs one.

Two wheelchairs! This is once again a situation no one in the hospital has anticipated. There are plenty of said chairs around, but no one available to push them other than an orderly. And all the orderlies are otherwise engaged, it being morning teatime.

The weeks turn into months, until at last both chairs and operators are unearthed. I feel the same heady freedom I experienced on being released from a Moroccan prison back in 1974. Perhaps it's the drugs. But finally the automatic doors open and I scent the fresh air of the outside world. I am heading home.

The drive home takes 25-minutes. During the time I've been in the hospital, someone has installed new bumps and potholes in the road. I feel every one of them.

Chapter 19
Catheterised

Did I mention that I am the proud possessor of a catheter? This is a cunning adaptation of a medieval torture device. As I have recently discovered, a fairly solid plastic tube is inserted through the tip of the penis and pushed up into the bladder. A balloon on the end of the device is then inflated with water to hold it in place.

The purpose of the catheter is not primarily the sadistic pleasure provided to the medical staff. Rather, it enables urine to drain from the bladder into a convenient bag. In fact, there are two bags—a 'leg bag' and a 'night bag'. They're as different as night and day.

As soon as I'm home, the good judge becomes my resident nurse. She has some difficulties at times with changing the catheter bags. They need to be emptied periodically. On one memorable occasion, she cannot get the leg bag unplugged. Her creative solution is to tug on the tube connected to my penis. That action certainly gains my attention.

On leaving the hospital, I'd been given a prescription for both Panadol and tramadol, but they haven't included any instructions on which is best to use, or whether they should be combined. I've certainly had Panadol before and am happy to take the maximum daily dosage.

I decide to look up tramadol and its side-effects. I get as far as reading that when used in association with alcohol, it can cause death. It's also highly addictive. Enough to convince me to stick with Panadol.

There's enough pain to convince me for the first 10 days or so of the need to lie on my back in bed. It's not my usual sleeping position. After a week of this, I began to feel like a hooker with a slipped disc. Except I'm not getting paid.

I sleep a lot. Sleep, read, and sleep again. I watch the new series of *Homeland*. And eat good food. Cognisant of the judge's culinary aversion, our friends and family undertake to deliver meals to us on a daily basis. And wonderful meals they are, too—made with love!

Chapter 20
Goodbye Dad

My father dies. He slipped out fairly peacefully after years of putting up a pretty good defence. The timing of his death is 11 days after my operation. Such events are blind to their convenience. It is incumbent on me to make my way down to Dunedin, especially because I'm the one who'll be conducting the funeral.

I hastily cancel an appointment to have my catheter removed, and the judge and I book flights. I'm still in pain but feel I can manage the journey okay. We decide to fly out of Hamilton's airport rather than Auckland's, to spare me the long drive.

The site for Hamilton's airport was carefully selected for its fog-inducing characteristics. Sure enough, as we approach the airfield, the previously clear sunny day grows murky with fog. We learn that our plane is currently circling above, unable to land. It circles for some thirty minutes before thinking better of it and going elsewhere.

With our flight cancelled, we face the prospect of competing with others for seats on other planes. It's apparent that we may not get to Dunedin in time for the funeral.

However, if we drive to Auckland, we can be booked onto the next available flight. Wearily, we get back in the car.

It seems a long day before we arrive in Dunedin. I'm still not allowed to drive, so the judge pilots our rental car to my aunt's house, where we'll be staying. As we drag our suitcases up the path, I trip on a flagstone and fall flat on my face. My surgeon must have been good at sewing because my wound stays intact—more so than my pride. I'm weary and sore and sorry for myself.

It could have been worse—my catheter bag might have burst! It should have been removed by now, but of course I had to miss the extraction because of the trip south. It's embarrassing to ask your host for a bucket in which to locate the overnight bag. Indignities, I've had a few…

We give my dad a good send-off. There are sausage rolls, which I consider the arbiter of whether a funeral is properly consummated or not. I'll always remember my father for his boyish grin, which was sufficient to forgive him a great deal. Afterwards, the judge and I find our weary way back home—without further catastrophe.

Chapter 21
A Load of Dribble

Three weeks out from the op, the catheter is at last removed. The hospital has called me in for an 8.30 a.m. appointment. The urology department, I conclude, has some similarities to a southern pleasure house. The first instruction is always to drop your trousers and get your tackle out.

My lovely assistant has me lie on the bed, on which she's placed a towel. She disconnects the leg bag from the catheter and then does something or other to deflate the balloon in my bladder. She advises me to take a deep breath, relax, and close my eyes.

I believe women are accustomed to such an invitation.

The nurse removes the sad balloon. I'm not sure how many people have had a few feet of rubber tubing and a balloon extracted through the tip of their penis, but it's not the sort of experience one easily forgets. My nurse does it with a flourish, like some sort of conjuring trick. Now you see it, now you don't.

A small stream of urine pursues the balloon down the urethra. I'd been advised to bring two pairs of trousers, but I'm currently not wearing any. Welcome to incontinence. Or perhaps welcome back, given that we're all born with it.

Speaking of which, I'm quickly handed a nappy to stem the dribble.

It's actually called a pad, and it fits snuggly inside your jockeys, pillowing the testicles in a soft bed of warmth. Except that occasionally the warmth comes in liquid form. I'm given a short lecture on the subject, complete with diagrams. But the question I really want to ask is not so much to do with the why as it is with when this bloody hell will stop.

Next up is a flow test. I stand over the cyber-toilet and piss like a goddam horse! The machine can't keep up with me, so gushing am I in my vigorous slash. I haven't urinated with this much enthusiasm since I was 18 or so. It's unexpected and glorious! No one can ever call me piss-poor again!

My nurse is surprised at the results and rather deflatingly suggests that what I have so generously sluiced away may be stomach fluids rather than urine. As if. She instructs me to pad-up and go for a walk around the hospital for half an hour, then return for further interrogation.

I suspect the idea is to see how much leakage will happen while I'm perambulating. I note the medical term is 'leakage' rather than 'pissing your pants'. However, I think I somewhat skew the results by virtue of pausing for a toilet stop on my tour, where number twos are in order. Yet again, needs must.

Still and all, when I find my way back for another flow test, I once again gush like a geyser, causing the little printing machine to go into a frenetic chatter. This outcome seems satisfactory to the examination board. After assurances that my leakage is minimal, I'm given a bag full of pads and shown the door.

While some people might regard wearing a form of nappies demeaning, I leave the hospital smiling like a home-detention prisoner whose ankle bracelet has been removed. I have progressed from pissing in a bag to pissing in my underpants. One small step for man, but a giant leap for my journey of recovery.

Chapter 22
The Long and the Short of It

One of the side effects of a prostatectomy is the shortening of the penis. My schlong has become short. There's some technical explanation for this state of affairs, but all I know is that I am now a little diminished. Not to mention the fact that my surgeon vigorously scraped out all the nerves responsible for instigating an erection.

My brain might be up for it at any given time, but my disco stick can provide nothing more than a flaccid sigh. A woody would not. Unlike the incontinence, this will be a permanent condition. The judge examines me (verbally rather than physically), wanting to know how I feel about this. Is my ego as deflated as my willy?

Surprisingly, the answer is no. I'd been forewarned, knew what was coming and that henceforth there would be no coming. We'd made good use of libido in the many years it was available, and now our intimacy would need to find a new form. On the plus side, I'd got to stay alive and share the presence of my wonderful wife.

There are other options, of course. The needle in the base of the penis is reputed to provide a bona fide boner. But for me, this solution offers the same inducement as a needle in the eye. I could take the blue pill (Viagra). But as a rheumatic fever survivor, I suspect it might give me a jolt in the wrong part of my anatomy.

It's interesting as a bloke to join the ranks of the castrati. Without putting too fine a point on it—or any point at all—I am impotent. My male ego should have shattered like that of an Australian losing at anything. I suppose I've reached an understanding that my identity as a man doesn't reside south of my waist. The core of my being is not to be found in my underpants.

But it's early days, and I live with the possibility that one night I might wake with a surprise to find my flag raised and waving in the wind. If faith healers can make a leg grow, surely they can lay hands on and extend my middle wicket. Someone might invent an implant that would give me a robocock. But I'm not holding my breath about that. Or my penis.

In generations gone by, at the age I am now I'd be dead. And there's not a lot of hanky panky in the grave, even when you and your partner are buried adjacent to each other. I'll trade length for longevity, given the options. I'll live without regret, preferring gratitude over attitude. A man is more than the sum of his parts. Or any one part in particular.

Chapter 23
Micturition Misery

Strange things happen. I begin getting up to pee four times in the night. It's painful. I suspect this is not right. Then I get feverish, alternating between hot and cold. Being a man, I ignore these symptoms in the solid conviction that everything will come right given time.

Everything gets worse.

I reach out to the urology department to see if I should be concerned. Their initial reaction is a rather grumpy rejoinder that I should concentrate on training my bladder. I've trained dogs in the past but never a bladder. Should I do it by rewarding good behaviour or punishing bad?

As an afterthought, they suggest I might consider an MSU. I try out various combinations to determine what this might be. Mad Soccer Umpire? Maladjusted Sedentary Uncle? Male Stripper Uniform? Eventually, Dr Google leads me to consider Mid-Stream Urine. This is a test, I learn, to be conducted by sampling the portion in between the beginning and the end of a wizz.

There doesn't seem to be any rationale as to why I should embark on such an exercise, so I think better of it.

Things get even worse. I'm sick and in pain. I toss and turn in bed. My fingers go white because there's no blood flowing through them. I wake at night drenched in sweat.

Perhaps it's the 'flu'? There comes the day when I succumb to familial pressure and totter along to do an MSU. Turns out I have a bladder infection. Turns out that 30 percent of people who have catheters for a long period of time get a UTI. For the men in the readership, UTI stands for urinary tract infection rather than unicorn tail infusion.

Somebody could have warned me. But nobody did. My night sweats have seen me wearing a swimming costume to bed and drifting in and out of convulsions. It's been worse than man flu. Antibiotics come to my aid but seem to spend their first three days considering their options. Finally, they get motivated and begin dealing to the UTI.

This is the final persuasion I need that God is a woman. I'm being punished for my lack of empathy for UTIs, which every member of the female species seems depressingly familiar with. I confess. I prost(r)ate myself in supplication for belittling the agony of a bladder infection. We, the mere males, have been woefully unsympathetic. We must do better.

During the whole of my journey of recovery, this has been the lowest moment. I've imagined the worst. Cancer cells hosting a jamboree in my bladder. The undertaker parking his hearse in the driveway. Father Time sharpening his sickle on the grindstone. The Sirens summoning me.

So, oh, how good it is when the first flicker of health makes its presence felt. Gradually, humanity returns, albeit patchily. I hear a bird singing outside my bedroom window, and it seems more of a hymn of praise than a funeral lament.

I feel the sap rising, not where it normally should, but in my very bones.

I get out of bed, begin cooking again, go walking, feel like a partially complete man. But I discover a new medical condition that I name BID—Bladder Infection Dread. Whenever I wake up feeling the need for the loo, I stay awake for hours deliberating on whether the condition has returned. I am BID-impaired. I wonder if there's a benefit for that.

PSA is another of those three-letter acronyms. I used to belong to the PSA when I was a Telecom linesman. The Public Service Association was a strong union back in the day. They were responsible for such generous measures as the provision of a brand-new pair of boots every six months. I still have a pair of them, 40 years later.

Recently, it's kiwifruit growers who've become more interested in PSA—*Pseudomonas syringae* pv. *actinidiae*. But of course you already knew that. This highly virulent disease can destroy vines and hence the fruit. As an invasive affliction that affects ovoid squishy capsules, it seems to me a good analogy for the PSA that is of most significance to me—Prostate Specific Antigen.

This version of PSA is a protein produced by the prostate gland. A simple blood test is used to measure its incidence. PSA levels in men with prostate cancer (which is a fair whack of us) are high and often on the increase. PSA is the canary in the mine that warns of possible cancer and usually indicates a need for the aforementioned DRE (or, in technical terms, finger up the bum).

So here I am awaiting the results of my first PSA test since the op. The desired result is zero. Anything higher than 0.02 indicates that the cancer has slipped the noose and is on the prowl. There's a certain amount of tension in the wait. It's like you've backed a horse and it's in the main bunch heading for the straight.

Strangely enough, I'm feeling great. It'll be a total shock to me if that feeling turns out to be an illusion and my pizzle-rot is silently spreading throughout my body. But then I was completely oblivious to the fact I had it in the first place. Somewhere in a lab, my results are being determined by a person in a white coat, unaware of their significance to me.

Chapter 24
Die Hard

I've just got off the phone from the doctor. The news is in. It's not good. My PSA is not only above zero, it is 7.4! In layman's terms, that means trouble. Is it a total shock, as I anticipated? Hell yes. The chances of a short distance to my finish line just increased. It looks like radiation treatment is back on the cards with a vengeance.

Those sneaky little bastard cancer cells have found their way into my bloodstream. Just when you think the coast is clear, they're at it again. No one expects the Spanish Inquisition. But I've got to ask my body what the hell is going on. I trusted you, I tell it, to kick in with all the immune cells you could muster, but we're not winning here. Just saying.

And as for you, you greasy little gobbling cancer parasites, hit me with your best shot! You'll need to be on your game to take me down. I'm a survivor. And I've got a legendary support team. I've walked through the shadows before and come out the other side into the sunlight.

There has been an element of stunned mullet silence on hearing the news, I confess. With no one around (the judge is at work) and nothing seeming very worthwhile, I turn to my email. A good friend who is hosting a radio show in Sydney has written with a link to her latest programme, which celebrates contemporary musicians on the theme of hope.

I have a listen, as much for distraction as anything. The first track is by Declan O'Rourke, an Irish muso. It's called *Be Brave and Believe.* The opening line, repeated, is "The first thing I want you to know is that everything is gonna be all right." It sizzles into my soul like a branding iron. The thing about synchronicity is that it makes you feel there might be more to life than what meets the eye.

Another coincidence is that the hospital has moved up my appointment with the radiologist. So there's only the weekend to get through before I learn more about my destiny. Things could be worse. I might have cancer. Oh yeah, that's right, I do. Well, another glass of wine then. What the hell!

The oncology department is a barrel of laughs. As I hand over my appointment letter to the receptionist, I can't help but notice a woman in the waiting room who seems a few cells short of a tumour.

She's shouting repeatedly, "Hurry up!" at the top of her voice.

The receptionist and I exchange eye rolls. I venture that the impatient patient is in the wrong place for that sentiment.

The judge and I compliantly take a seat, and then are greatly cheered by the arrival of Tiffany, who has come to support us. She alone is worth the entire budget of Vote Health, at least from my perspective. Within 10 minutes, she's told us everything we need to know and answered the judge's questions clearly and compassionately.

Sadly, we still need to get the same information repeated to us, once by a registrar, and then by a consultant. Jimmy the registrar is a convivial chap, but quickly assumes a serious face to indicate that he's not treating us lightly. For my own part, I'm happy to continue the light-hearted banter, even though the subject matter is supposedly grave, if not the grave.

After reviewing my case notes, interrogating me on my medical history, and examining my scar, Jimmy is satisfied that he's not sure what to suggest. He takes his indecisiveness off to the consultant, who, like the Wizard of Oz, is temporarily concealed from us. Eventually the two of them return, with a medical student in tow.

Roger, the consultant, has a very sharp suit. He is permanently sombre, even when I crack jokes. I think he's of the opinion that I'm not taking my imminent demise seriously enough. I don't feel inclined to explain that I completely understand the gravity of the situation, but I'll be buggered if I'm going to let it ruin my day.

While I've expected that radiation will be the outcome of the meeting, Roger is not sure it's warranted. The problem, he explains, is that the oncology team can't make sense of my elevated PSA score. Join the club. With a great deal of sober commentary, he tells us they don't know enough to know anything. However, it seems there are three possibilities.

One, there's a bit of cancerous material left in my pelvic region. If that's the case, it'll be good news. Two, cancer may be residing in some of my lymph nodes. And, three, the cancer could be touring my veins, looking for a place to call home. The latter two possibilities are, as they say, undesirable.

The plan now is to send me back through the scanners—an MRI and a CT. The oncologists hope the scans might reveal something but warn they probably won't. In which case, they may proceed with a treatment called an SFA.

Essentially, though, it seems they can't treat what they can't find.

My take on all this is that, in the medicos' professional opinion, I'm fucked. I beg to differ. I have promises to keep and miles to go before I sleep. The judge and I make our way home. She's a tad shaky on it, and we hold each other for a while. We opt for Indian takeaways and open another bottle of wine. Our toast to each other is the Jewish one—"*L'chaim!*"—to life.

Chapter 25
Night Terrors

I've got pain in my lower back. It started when I was scooping leaves from the bottom of our swimming pool. I've had weakness there (in my back rather than the pool) ever since my spine got chipped when I was playing rugby many years ago. Apparently, the chip is still floating around in the spinal fluid somewhere.

From time to time, while doing a little strenuous exercise, my back protests and the surrounding muscles go into spasm. Worst case, I can't walk for a while. But mostly, with a few magic pills, it all comes right within about a week. The problem is I did whatever I did two weeks ago and my back is still aching.

What you need to know in relation to this is that the judge had earlier asked the consultant what the first sign would be if my cancer had spread.

"Pain in the lower back," he said cheerily.

So now, if I wake at night with my spine aching, I assume that I'm lousy with cancer and might as well call it quits.

The night terrors are the most chilling of them all. Rationality doesn't count for snatch in the early hours of the morning. It's a time for considering funeral hymns and choosing between burial and cremation. Roasting on the grill of my imagination, I'm completely alone in the universe. Death hovers over me with a measuring tape.

The first coffee of the morning provides a miraculous cure. Oh, the wondrous curative properties of caffeine! It ignites the fires of consciousness, which in turn dispel the spectral demons of the night. Maybe I'll go one more round of chancing my existence in this world of opportunities.

Cancer is a friend magnet. All sorts of people suddenly want to come and visit. Dear people, who have been part of my stumbling journey through life. They find all sorts of excuses, but I guess there's a shadow in their hearts suggesting they get in early in case I don't make it out the other side. That's just fine with me.

It's kind of useful to be able to play the cancer card. I can use it to excuse bad behaviour and jump ahead in the queue. If I have a mind to, I dare say I can slouch around in bed all day and have cups of tea brought to me. On the other hand, the judge knows me too well and that she can still expect dinner to be on the table when she gets home.

On a Friday, I make the cavalier decision to abandon incontinence pads. Doing this may seem a small advance, but to me it's a huge liberation to be out of nappies. Almost makes me feel adult. So far, so good. I haven't pissed my pants once, even when the All Blacks pulled off a historic win. I'm of sound bladder, whatever state the rest of me may be in.

I have my next CT scan. Pity the poor CT machine. Everyone knows a self-respecting piece of medical equipment has at least three letters to its name. Like the majestic MRI scanner or the supersonic PET replicator. Still and all, the CT does have a half-arsed 'O' ring with a few flashing lights and whirring sounds.

The best bit about it is that it gives me a clear result. Having searched for metastatic disease, it finds zilch. To quote the less than voluminous report, there is 'no evidence of new suspicious lesions'. I'll take that. Though it's a little early to celebrate. There's still the *Star Trek* teleporter (aka MRI) to come, with its superior imaging hopefully revealing all.

Maybe CT stands for 'completely trustworthy'. Or not. It could be 'curiously treacherous'. These are the idle neuroses of the cancer patient. Being endlessly tested is a combination of hoping for the best and preparing for the worst. It's a process laden with destiny but unremitting in its impartiality. None of my tests thus far have been susceptible to magical thinking.

But then neither have my Lotto tickets, and I keep buying them. At some point in the cancer journey, it's beneficial to accept the fact that neither magic potions nor positive thinking nor ghastly diets nor religious incantations have any effect on the rapidly dividing rogue cells. I could say all this makes me feel impotent, except I am impotent already.

The people who love you need to believe there's something they can do to help. What I appreciate about this is not so much their invocations or sage advice, but the fact that these are signs that they love me and don't want to lose me. While trying not to carry their burden along with my own, I'm grateful for their presence and commitment.

The journey would be a long and lonely one to make alone. Instead, I feel supported, not only by my padless undies but by a wonderful community of wife, family, friends, medical staff, and anonymous sycophants. In a strange encounter outside a restaurant last night, I met someone I'd not talked to in the last six months. She knew everything about my condition. Go figure.

Just like waking up each morning, it's better than the alternative.

Chapter 26
MRI

The MRI scan takes place on a Monday, and I hope I'll get the results by the end of the week. But 5 p.m. Friday comes around, and I resign myself to another weekend of uncertainty. I set out the items for our G&Ts and go scavenging in our local town for the Friday offering of fish and chips.

By the time I get home, there's an email notifying me that new lab results have been posted on my online portal. Without too much expectation, I log in and am surprised to see the heading MRI Scan Results. There's that moment of dread when you place the cursor over the link and wonder whether you really want to learn your destiny.

I click. No medical report has ever been famous for its lucid clarity. This one contains such everyday words as adenocarcinoma, anastomosis, deononvilliers, cirrhosis, sigmoid, mesorectal, and lymphadenopathy. Surely that can't be good. And then, finally, I discover the summary statement that needs no translation.

It reads, "Seminal vesicles region affected but nil else." I've never been so excited to learn that a scan has detected cancer! This is the best possible result I could have hoped for.

It explains entirely the high marks I got in the PSA test. There's a little bit of cancerous tissue left where the surgeon thought it might be.

In the game of *Where's Wally?* Wally has been located. Wally is just basking in the pelvic bed, waiting to be zapped with radiation. There's no evidence of the cancer having spread anywhere else. I've dodged a potentially fatal bullet. And while there will no doubt be further treatment to get me completely out of the woods, the road ahead has opened up considerably.

I read the report through a few dozen times to make sure I've got it right. I'm prepared to forgive the somewhat unnecessary observation that "the rectum and sigmoid shows marked faecal loading." I don't give a shit! This is better news than winning Lotto. Of course, I never doubted it. Well, okay, maybe a few hundred times.

I ring our daughters, both of whom cry with me. And then I email the news to our supporters' group. Immediately there's a flood of relief and encouragement spilling into my inbox. The judge immediately starts planning to work past her official retirement age, by way of celebration. Some people get their kicks in strange ways.

Chapter 27
Valley of the Shadow

Dead man walking. A few days later we reel out of a meeting with the oncologist who's been perusing the same results that gave us such good cheer. He's explained that the 'residual disease' they've located is in such a tricky position that neither radiation nor surgery can treat it without greatly diminishing my quality of life.

The only possibility is 'expectant waiting', which is a medical euphemism for doing nothing. When the judge incisively drives to the heart of the matter, the oncologist gives me between one and two years left to live. While I have a hunger for information, this is not the sort of verdict I had in mind.

We stumble to the hospital café, where we look at each other and weep into our Earl Grey tea. Back home, we take a long walk around the lake, holding hands all the way. It was how we first came to love each other 43 years ago—walking and talking. There have been many shadows across our path in that time, but this one is the darkest.

I have phone conversations with all my children to let them know before sending out a generic email. When I convey the doctors' decision to my eldest daughter, she responds with the classic line, "How fucking dare they!" She is adamant that I will live and reminds me not to accept an opinion as inevitability.

What do you do with a death sentence? Accept it or reject it? Fear it or ignore it? My own preference is not to give it oxygen. I am not my cancer. Life is not a possession but a gift. I come from a long line of survivors who have been written off at different points in their lives. Each day I wake is wonderful. I am alive! And I'll stay that way while I can.

At the same time, I cover my bases. I need to revise my will and prepare instructions so that the judge will have confidence in negotiating the many details that I currently take care of. And I give early notice of a celebratory occasion to be held in the coming months. It will take the form of a Fuck Cancer party.

In the meantime, suggestions for possible cures flood in from friends and acquaintances. How can it be that cancer has not already been swept away when there are so many folk remedies with proven effects? These good people want to offer hope to me. But I find myself dazed and pressured, as if I am somehow wilfully neglecting obvious solutions.

In my worst moments, I'm just glad that I didn't go to the expense of getting my teeth whitened. Hopefully, in a coffin, I'll have my mouth closed. Perversely, I continue to feel healthy and active. We're all only a few minutes away from death at any time. It's just that medical experts have opined as to my future longevity.

Well, as my daughter said, "How fucking dare they?"

Chapter 28
Life Before Death

Everyone around me is muttering in whispers. They look at me with a mixture of compassion and alarm. I find myself needing to constantly jolly them along. I remind them I'm not quite dead yet—just having a bad day. It's not over until the Fat Lady sits on my coffin. In rugby, you have to keep playing until after the hooter sounds.

In the meantime, I'm in a state of ignorant joy. It's spring, my favourite time of the year. Bleak dead branches start erupting with tiny buds that will become verdant green leaves. As James Michener wrote in *The Fires of Spring*, "In spring, of course, any place is beautiful, because in spring fires leap from your heart, and you can see things that aren't there."

Maybe cancer cells are replicating in my bone marrow as I write, but all I can feel is gratitude for the beauty that surrounds me. I'm currently reading *The Choice* by Edith Eger. She tells the story that in the women's barracks of Auschwitz, the women bared their breasts one night and had a titty contest. Edith won on points.

One of my best friends died of prostate cancer back in 2004. I went to visit him a few days before he shuffled off. He wasn't looking too flash. His dog lay beside him on the bed.

The son of a Welsh poet, Tom was a hell-raiser and a pioneer. He lived fully and died asking questions. He invented a name for God: Umbra Major—The Great Shadow.

Before Tom died, he organised for 5000 tulip bulbs and 10,000 daffodil bulbs and wildflowers to be planted around his mountain home. He knew he wouldn't live to see them. It didn't matter. He was invested in life and wanted to leave something beautiful for others. Such an investment is a form of guerrilla warfare for love.

In the midst of my own struggles, I take on responsibility for managing the installation of a new kitchen. Today the workers didn't come again, marking six weeks that I've had to wash dishes in the bathroom basin. I suddenly lose the plot and swear at the project manager. And then I cry. Sometimes you just have to ride the waves. Joy and grief are close companions.

Back in my 30s, I did an exercise that required drawing a timeline from the present to death. It was a way of focusing on what you wanted to achieve before the full stop. In many ways, I've exceeded what I aimed for. But on current projections, the line will stop significantly short of my expectations. I imagine there're no refunds.

But for now, my darling grandson has come to hang out. And his mother, our youngest daughter, is pregnant again. These are things to live for. Life goes on relentlessly, whether we're riding the merry-go-round or not. It seems to me it's the awareness of moments that counts rather than the accumulation of years. No point in life after death if there's no life before death.

Chapter 29
Desperately Seeking Solutions

There's a thing called a NanoKnife machine. Very *Star Trek*. It's used for treating prostate cancer tumours by inserting needles adjacent to the offending tissue and blasting it with electric current. It's been around for a while but has only just made it to New Zealand. Might it work where surgery can't? I decide to check it out. Worth a throw of the dice.

It's kinda like ECT for sad cells. Hit them with your best volts. I've already had a pelvic frontal lobotomy, so it's time for the next cab off the rank.

In truth, I'm very confused. I'd like nothing more than for my immune system to spark up and cull the rogue cells without any need for further intervention.

To that end, I'm taking selenium supplements and massive doses of vitamin C—soon to be delivered intravenously. I continue my daily practice of meditation and prayer and the gentle exercise of walking.

All of this may seem like I'm clutching at straws. But at least I'm not yet at the point of apricot kernels or pineapple stems. I have my dignity, or at least my epicurean taste buds.

To what lengths should a person go to preserve their life? Are there any limits? Or is any self-imposed boundary evidence of a lack of love for those with a vested interest? These are lonely ponderings, and I crave the space and silence to pursue them without intimidation.

The survival instinct is strong. I want to live, to enjoy some autumnal years, to see my grandchildren grow, and to spend more time with the judge. But not at any cost. I want to live well, not just exist in pain and discomfort.

To which a quiet voice replies, "You are living well. What more do you want?"

Ah well. That win on the Lotto would still be nice. I suppose a miraculous erection might be pushing the boundaries.

The irony is that I can't, in all honesty, suggest that I want to live with a certain future. None of us have that. We have this moment we exist in. It'll have to do.

Chapter 30
Hit Me with It!

I'm reading *The Emperor of All Maladies* by Siddhartha Mukherjee. It's subtitled *A Biography of Cancer* and reads like a medical *House of Cards*. These pioneer physicians are a cross between geniuses and demented crusaders on a holy war.

The worst of them are obsessive narcissists, determined to be the first to conquer the invasive demon. They excise flesh as if it were the enemy. They up the doses of chemical poison, driving patients to an early death. They fire radiation into tissue until it has fried and died.

But the best of them take the time to learn and to think. They are the detective doctors, listening for the secrets of cellular whispers. Such investigators realise they're dealing with mysteries and try to penetrate to the heart of the alien that confronts them. It's a journey of understanding that demands a certain respect.

And like all successful pioneers, they're prepared to listen. Shunning the petty infighting of medical empires, these explorers prospect for information wherever they find it—including the stories of the patients themselves. They forgo their assumptions in the interests of learning.

We, the guinea pigs, find ourselves in a quicksand of half-arsed opinions. The literature is chock full of expert wrong calls on both sides of the equation. With luck and a fair wind, a cancer patient can defy the odds by years or even completely. Or they may fall down dead—either despite of or because of the treatments offered.

While scattering my father's ashes in his hometown, I made myself a resolution. I'm going to live till at least 70. Once there, I'll review my options. How I'm going to achieve this goal, I have no idea. But I figure it's a better strategy than curling up my toes and accepting Roger's bleak prediction.

The pain in my back is not muscular. It now wakes me in the night. The chances are it's a sign that the cancer has spread to the pelvic bones. Or not. I'm not sure if I want to know. What can I do about it if it has? Complain? I prefer to suck it up and carry on regardless.

I'm on a run at the moment. My phone died completely, mid-text. The kitchen installers placed a gas hob in a position that breaches building regulations. The guys laying the vinyl suddenly found that the one we'd ordered was discontinued. My daughter had a miscarriage at 10 weeks.

First-world problems, I know. But sometimes you get the feeling that the universe is just lined up against you. Best to stay in bed all day, except that would make my back hurt. So I take the other option. I laugh in the face of it. Fuck you, I say. Here I am, still breathing. What else you got?

Chapter 31
UTI

Nobody expects the *return* of the Spanish Inquisition. It's a holiday weekend, and I'm cooking for family. Suddenly I feel cold and begin shaking. An hour or so later, I'm sweating, and my temperature is shooting for glory. For the next few days, I vacillate between these states, with random periods of calm.

I'm not sure what the hell it's all about. Then on Monday, when, of course, doctors' surgeries are still closed, there's a couple of spots of blood in my urine. I've been repossessed by the UTI demon! The next day my self-diagnosis is confirmed, and I begin a course of antibiotics.

That night everything gets worse than worse. Every part of me aches, my temperature rockets, and I wake in a literal pool of sweat. I'm not sure I'll make it through the night. I'd be quite happy not to. I take pills of every sort, but still I'm awake, cooking slowly on the torturous grill. This is the sickest I've ever been in my life. Even with man flu.

But, as they say, every silver lining has a cloud. Friends of ours come to visit, and Richard is a paediatrician. He listens to the story of my dalliance with cancer and raises a few pertinent questions. He's as dubious as I am about my looming sentence of death and offers to go into bat for me in terms of getting a second opinion.

Within a matter of days, he's hooked me up with an associate professor of radiation oncology who is happy to look at my notes and review my case. Turns out that we attended the same school, the motto of which is *Altiora Peto*—Seek Higher Things. Back in the day, this epithet was motivation for urinal competitions at the single-sex college.

In conjunction with this orthodox approach, I'm pushing the boat out with a few Looney Tunes therapies. A week ago, I visited a qualified doctor who specialises in integrative medicine. He was upfront in terms of acknowledging that he didn't know how to cure cancer. Instead, he concentrates on stimulating the body's immune system to kick into gear.

Consequently, I'm about to embark on intravenous vitamin C treatment twice a week. I'm also taking turmeric tablets and a vitamin D3 supplement. It's a deeply scientific regime known as the shotgun approach. Fire everything you have in both barrels in the hope that something might work. Who knows when your luck might change?

Chapter 32
Strangely Satisfying

I wake in the middle of the night with an unanticipated problem. I've had a wet dream. TMI, I know, but I didn't imagine this was possible. When I say I'm having a wet dream, it's the equivalent of saying the Amazon River is a wee trickle. Somehow, I'm spurting like an epileptic fire hose, drenching everything in sight.

It's strangely satisfying. At least, a small part of my apparatus must still be working. But it also leaves me lying in a pool of sticky substance. I have to go find a towel to lie on. Did I have an erection while dousing whatever blaze I was fighting? I can't remember, and anyway, it's physically impossible, so probably not. I lie awake, remembering more virile times.

Since you asked, no, I haven't felt less complete as a man since forcibly losing my woody powers. Maybe it's because I'm 64 (will you still need me?). Despite the perpetual adolescent fantasy, it seems there's more to being male than getting your rocks off. And if it comes to a choice between me remaining upright as opposed to my prime member, I choose life.

Believe it or not, there is such a thing as intimacy without orgasm. I know that seems like a piece of female propaganda, but it turns out it's true. The judge and I hug at night with a sense of completion that carries all those years of lovemaking and trust within it. And neither of us is in the mood for making babies, as it happens.

In the meantime, the vitamin C infusions are underway, twice a week. Each visit makes a hole in my available time, given that the drip takes 1.5 hours to complete and then an hour's travel time on top. And an even bigger hole in my wallet. Still and all, I get to spend some of my weekdays on a recliner chair, reading a book in peace and quiet. Good work if you can get it.

Do the infusions work? Who knows? I certainly don't feel any worse off, and they do no harm. I'm still feeling in fine fettle. And it was after a couple of treatments that my fire hydrant erupted. So maybe they do have welcome side-effects.

I couldn't possibly comment.

Chapter 33
Back to Basics

Opinions, there've been a few...The NanoKnife people keep promising to report but never do. In the end, the judge rings and demands an answer. They apologise and confess there is nothing they can do. So much for *Star Trek* solutions. I guess I'll have to wait for the next millennium.

But my man in Christchurch comes through. We have a phone conference. He's direct, compassionate, and clear. He confirms that neither surgery nor radiation therapy is a viable option. Because we went to the same school, he gives me advice as if speaking to his younger brother, in whom he has a vested interest. I appreciate it.

What then are the options? Well, back to the basics—it's living or dying. I still prefer the former, all things considered. He suggests hormone treatment as a way of buying a couple of years to see what develops in the research field. Being a respectable medical option, this one of course has three letters. It's known as ADT, or Androgen Deprivation Therapy.

Androgen (or Andy, as he's known by his mates) is best known as the producer of testosterone. And testosterone is the raw fuel of prostate cancer. In days gone by, the preferred solution to dampen down the flames was an orchidectomy. While this might sound like a horticultural technique to produce fine blooms, it's actually surgical castration, which stops the production of testosterone.

So the alternative is chemical castration, or ADT. I've been downright resistant to taking the stuff. Why? Because of the side-effects. There's an 81 percent increase in cardiovascular risk (stroke or heart attack). Also, bone-thinning, weight gain, growth of breasts, depression, hot flushes, memory loss, and an interest in lingerie. Okay, I made the last one up.

But as a promotional write-up, it's less than convincing. The plus side is that it slows the growth of the cancer for maybe two years, until the disease develops resistance to it. I'm already resistant to it, and I'm not even on it yet. I come back to the quantity- versus quality-of-life dilemma. Is the game worth the candle?

While I consider the feminine aspects of my personality well-developed in comparison to some of my more macho gender-buddies, I've never had any desire to fondle my own breasts. Nor to experience menopause, which for me would translate directly into pausing being a man. Ah, the many options that open up when one has prostate cancer!

Oh, I forgot to mention that erectile dysfunction is another side effect. But I've already got that. And if, I wonder, I start taking ADT, will I then become susceptible to breast cancer? At least women's health is better funded than men's. I need to make my mind up on which way to go instead of continually vacillating. Maybe I've already become female?

Yet another of the interminable PSA tests comes in with a score of 21.4. It's jumped by 10 in just over a week. I decide to rename PSA as Potential Survival Alert. That way I can take it as positive news—21 has to be twice as good as 10, right? I'm tempted to have a 21st party. But even I don't fool myself. Something's going on down there, even if I'm not aware of it on a daily basis. Something's wonky ponk alright.

On the positive side, I cancel the vitamin C treatments. They may not be doing any harm, but they're clearly not doing any good either. The cancellation saves me $400 a week. I'm feeling better already.

Fortunately, the latest PSA news comes in the same week that I have a meeting scheduled with my tag team of Glen and Tiffany back at Waikato Hospital. We're approaching decision time, when I need to decide whether to sacrifice my masculinity on the altar of longevity. What would you do?

There's only one item on the agenda when we meet, at least to start with. Which form of castration will I opt for? Chemical or surgical? It's like the last two chocolates in the box—hard to choose between them. I'm inclining towards the chop. Whip my balls off, why don't you? It might give me a new career as a soprano. Glen treats this as a viable option (the surgery, not the singing). But he gently persuades me that I should have a trial run with the ADT to see how it goes.

Having a short-term trial (three months) sounds like a good option. Except I haven't quite realised he means here and now. Before long, a nurse is inserting a scarily big needle into my stomach. Through it, she injects a slow-release device in my abdomen to dispense Zoladex, which will mop up my testosterone over the next three months. That's it, then.

Glen is wondering if I shouldn't also have an early dose of chemo, just to knock things around a little. So he organises an appointment with an oncologist to see if that's a goer. On the plus side, most of my hair has already fallen out, and I know how to rock a hat. I'm not so keen on vomiting, but I guess you get used to anything.

Chapter 34
The Final Chapter

It seems a long time down the track since my dribbly urine stream gave way to a cancer diagnosis. Last Christmas, I was a healthy virile man with a long, indolent future ahead of me. As this one approaches, I bear urinary stigmata, have the erectile performance of a slug on barbiturates, am growing breasts, and all I have to look forward to is throwing up my Christmas dinner.

There is no hope of a cure, according to The Powers That Be. Technically, my treatment is in the realm of palliative care—something that makes a problem seem less serious but does not solve the problem. I'm on life support, but there are no machines to switch off. So far, it's not just the length of my penis that's been foreshortened.

Stubborn bastard that I am, I'm not inclined to take my imminent demise as a given. All my life I've played the odds and occasionally beaten them. Unfortunately, not in regard to Lotto. But my son has taught me the value of the small phrase, "Nothing is impossible." There are two types of people in the world—gamblers and bureaucrats.

The task ahead of me is to string my life out like a tantric sex session. If I don't die of the treatment, I might live from sheer bloody-mindedness. Few things are as enjoyable as proving the experts wrong. I once wrote a novel with a sex scene that lasted 13 pages. Then I made a feature film of the book that everyone agreed could not be made. This time I just want to make a good 10 years.

That being the case, I don't think I can string out this interminable account of my adventure for another decade. It's time to bring the thing to an end (which is what my doctors seem to be saying to me). But how to conclude it? While it may seem there are only two possible outcomes, the judge treats as divine law the maxim that there are always three options.

That being decreed, I have decided to offer you three possible conclusions from which to choose. You can pick whichever you feel is the most likely or appealing. After all, you have as much chance of knowing as I have. So here we go—a trifecta of finales. As my wife is fond of saying, you be the judge.

Otago Daily Times, 27 June 2018
Robert Michael Riddell (1953–2018)

Ex-Dunedin resident and writer Mike Riddell passed away on 19 June after a brief struggle with prostate cancer. Riddell taught at the University of Otago from 2001–2003. He was the author of novels *The Insatiable Moon* (which he later adapted for the screen) and *Masks & Shadows*, among many other books.

Riddell also wrote and produced the play *Jerusalem, Jerusalem* about the final days of James K. Baxter. This

Dunedin production, performed at the Globe, toured New Zealand and featured at the Edinburgh Fringe Festival in 2003, where the sister-city relationship with Dunedin was celebrated. It was directed by his wife, Rosemary, a former lawyer and now district court judge. She also directed *The Insatiable Moon* for the screen.

Mike was the screenwriter for *The Guinea Pig Club,* a film, directed by Roger Donaldson, about Dunedin-born plastic surgeon Sir Archibald McIndoe,

During his time in Dunedin, Riddell founded the network *Screen Dunedin*, was a board member of the Dunedin Fringe Festival, and managed the inaugural Otago *48 Hours* film festival. He completed a doctorate at the University of Otago on the spirituality of James K. Baxter. Riddell is survived by Rosemary and their children Matthew, Anna, and Katherine.

At his funeral, a special plea was made for increasing awareness of prostate cancer. In a statement written before his death, Riddell suggested that men are sadly remiss in confronting health issues. He described prostate cancer as a sleeping assassin and advised all men to consult their doctor whenever things were 'wonky ponk down under'.

In place of a voluntary at the conclusion of the service, a recording was played of Leonard Cohen singing *Bird on a Wire*.

Buzz Mag, 28 March 2028
Ten Minutes with…Mike Riddell

We caught up with author and screenwriter Mike Riddell during a brief visit to his homeland to speak at the Auckland Readers and Writers Festival. These days he and his wife

Rosemary spend most of their time in their apartment in the south of France. *Buzz* had a few questions for him.

It may be a dumb question, but why France?

Why not? We'll always be Kiwis at heart, but the French culture and aesthetic have long held a special attraction for us. My wife and I are in that stage of life when we're free to travel, and a base in France makes it easier for us. We had no intention of settling there, but one day we came across a fabulous apartment in Haut-de-Cagnes and bought it. It was pure impulse—the way we usually do things. We still have a small bolthole here in Auckland.

What are you speaking on at the festival?

The main focus will be on my latest film, *Billy*, which is still in development. It's a biopic about Billy Preston. Shooting wrapped a few weeks ago, but I haven't seen the rushes yet. So I'll be talking about the process of writing for a biopic. It's always a challenge and a gift to be presented with the raw material of a person's life and to try to uncover a story that tells the truth about him or her. Preston was an intriguing figure, and I think audience will fall in love with him.

It might be a little indelicate, but you're 75 now…

Just! I turned 75 last week…Thanks for revealing that to the world!

You're welcome. Anyway, the question is, are you planning to stop writing any time soon?

Well, I'm not planning to, but I expect that I'll stop writing about the same time as I stop breathing. Writing isn't so much a job as it's a vocation. A writer writes, as they say. I can't imagine a life without it. For me, it's a way of processing experience—I'm never sure what I think until I've put it on paper. The short answer is that I'm nervous about ceasing, in case it results in the ultimate cessation.

You seem in good health now, but I understand you had a brush with cancer a few years back?

Indeed, I did. In 2017, I was diagnosed with a particularly aggressive form of prostate cancer and given just a couple of years to live. As you can see, I seem to have confounded that prediction. I think it was a combination of some good medical advice back then and the advances in treatment that came through in the nick of time. Together with the fact that I'm a cantankerous old bastard, and I wasn't quite ready to die.

What are you working on currently?

Writers are always reluctant to talk about their latest projects for fear they'll jinx them. Suffice it to say that I'm deep in the midst of a third draft for yet another biopic and also fiddling around with another novel.

All the best with that, and we look forward to your session at the festival, which I believe is this Saturday.

Which also happens to be the first of April, so anything could happen!

Waikato Times, 19 September 2019
Tragic Accident

An investigation into the death of a man in the precinct of Waikato Hospital has found no liability and is being described as a tragic accident. The report into the events of 10 August found no culpability on the part of the driver of the vehicle, a St Johns ambulance.

Mike Riddell (66), a resident of Cambridge, was struck by the ambulance as it approached the accident and emergency department of the hospital. According to witness reports, the victim appeared distracted as he stepped off the kerb into the path of the speeding vehicle.

Ambulance driver Katrina Roberts told the *Waikato Times* that she had no time to react. The paramedic team had been transporting a woman with a critical heart event when the accident occurred.

"We were in a hurry," said Roberts, "but were proceeding with care."

The siren had been turned off in keeping with hospital policy during the final approach.

Ironically, the man killed was there for an appointment with his cancer consultant, Dr Sam Bailey.

"I'd just given him the very good news that he was clear of prostate cancer," said Dr Bailey. "He was part of a clinical trial of a new medication, and we were all excited for him that he now had a clean bill of health."

The doctor declined to comment as to whether this news had distracted the victim.

No further inquiry is to be undertaken by police, who are satisfied with their own and the hospital's investigations.

The wife of the deceased, Judge Rosemary Riddell, accepted the report, admitting that her former husband could be a bit inattentive at times.

When approached for her feelings about the unfortunate chain of events, she commented, "Shit happens."

Acknowledgements

It's strange for a book to acknowledge the author. But my darling husband Mike deserves my thanks for how he wrestled with prostate cancer but also got on with life in such a determined way.

One day, a year or so after Mike's death, I found myself trying to make sense of all the documents on his computer. That's when I discovered the manuscript of this book. I began reading it, immediately engaged by the humour and bigheartedness that leapt from every page. I gave it to friends to read. They too were entranced, which prompted me to consider if the book merited publication. I decided it did, and the rest as they say is history.

Mike was a gifted writer, an environmentalist and a committed father to Matthew, the late Polly and Katherine. I'm proud to have known and loved him.

I also want to acknowledge Marion Yule, whose catchphrase inspired the title of this book, and also Gair Cook for his brilliantly executed cartoons.

I am especially indebted to the people in Oturehua, the small village where I live, who have surrounded me with support and friendship from the time Mike and I moved there in 2018. In particular, thank you to my friend and editor Paula Wagemaker for her advice and assistance with this book.

– Rosemary Riddell
Oturehua, New Zealand, 2024